LIVING AND DYING
IN A MIND FIELD

TOADHOUSE, a.k.a. Allan Graham, was born in San Francisco, California, in 1943. He is an artist whose work includes sculpture, painting, words, and video.

Language is a virus from outer-space.

William S. Burroughs
The Ticket that Exploded

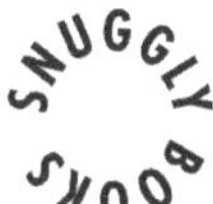

The famous black hat will perform in
square yards—it will take just as long
being visually critical laying on your back
facing forward . . .

she took off her socks to put others
on—a woman with her father possibly
old—reality is our short coming a
technical look that refuses forgiveness
pink is fontly reminiscent

appearance
deforms
mirrors

knows
falls
from
face

ephemeral
eternally

flesh
sets
the tone

**COGNITIVE
RETURNS DIMINISHING
WITH DILAPIDATED
PROFUSION**

(many have plundered this hole)

TAKE—
A RED ROUND RUBBER
ROOSTER
TO A
free-range
feathered ball

life
in
a
nut
shell[1]

____

1. In the end we are all jerky!

at some point put . . .

**DEAD
PAN**

in a box . . .

RELUCTANCE
TAILORED FOR
FUTURE
WALLS

OIL & WATER ARE RELATIVE
DISCrEPENCIES—
TEARS ARE SOLVENT &
THE WIND TAKES YOUR
BREATH
AWAY . . . .

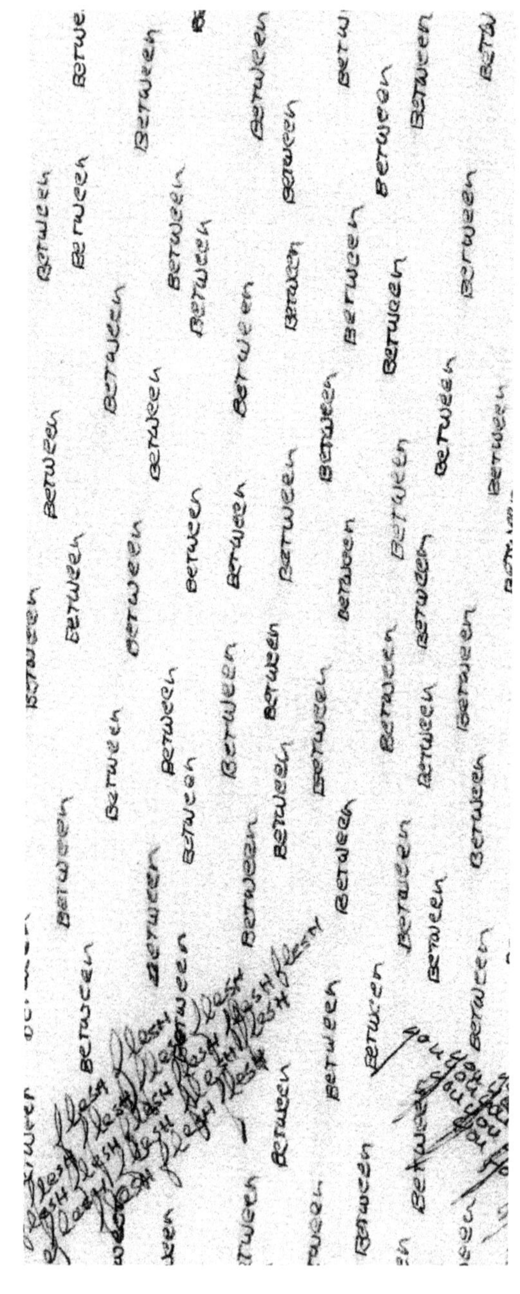

t
h
o
u
g
h
t
i
s
p
a
r
e
n
t
h
e
t
i
c
a
l
s
p
a
c
e

Words buttered inside and out. Toast on the side. Thought is extremely touchy toward description. Naivety walks in its shadow—conforming to its wake. Life is the reconfiguring of abstraction.

we are the outcome of abstraction . . .
breath, mind, meandering edges and
Sensuality set to music.

The world is not literal—take my word
for it!

**DEAD
PAN**

UFO-isms

thought & limit in an is galaxy
the great spiral nebula me in a we universe
three ones passing through a binary system
from & form in an if shower
light passing through an un formation
breeze & finger approaching an ado galaxy
once in a too system
surface

The way to the front is from the back.
Movement is the instant passed on.

<u>Possible UFOs</u>

nothing	is
flesh	outside
between	inside
you	identity
direction	ones
seed	change
empty	form
distance	mind
surface	thought
need	limit
chance	me
beyond	we
(0)	living
	dying
	fear
	shadows
	good
	bad
	it
	if
	distance
	wink
	stone

Possible UFOs

name	(½)
stick	light
be	breeze
to	finger
from	???
un	once
memory	too
meaning	to
silence	surface
etc.	was
fish	isn't
hill	thought
stream	limit
plus	other
minus	opposite
non	charge
tongue	edge
lips	drift
soft	why
odd	center
even	self
either	even
enigma	same

NO
THY
SELF[1]

---

1. prosthetic hear

A man is discussing something with his
hands. A trite cosmic reality. Culture
serves time.

eliminate the distance between points

take time out

affordable self shortage

local distribution of the present

back of the cantalope cranial foreplay

grass milks cows nose

be a front for a back

approaching as if there was a place

the dreams that I have never had I can
only imagine

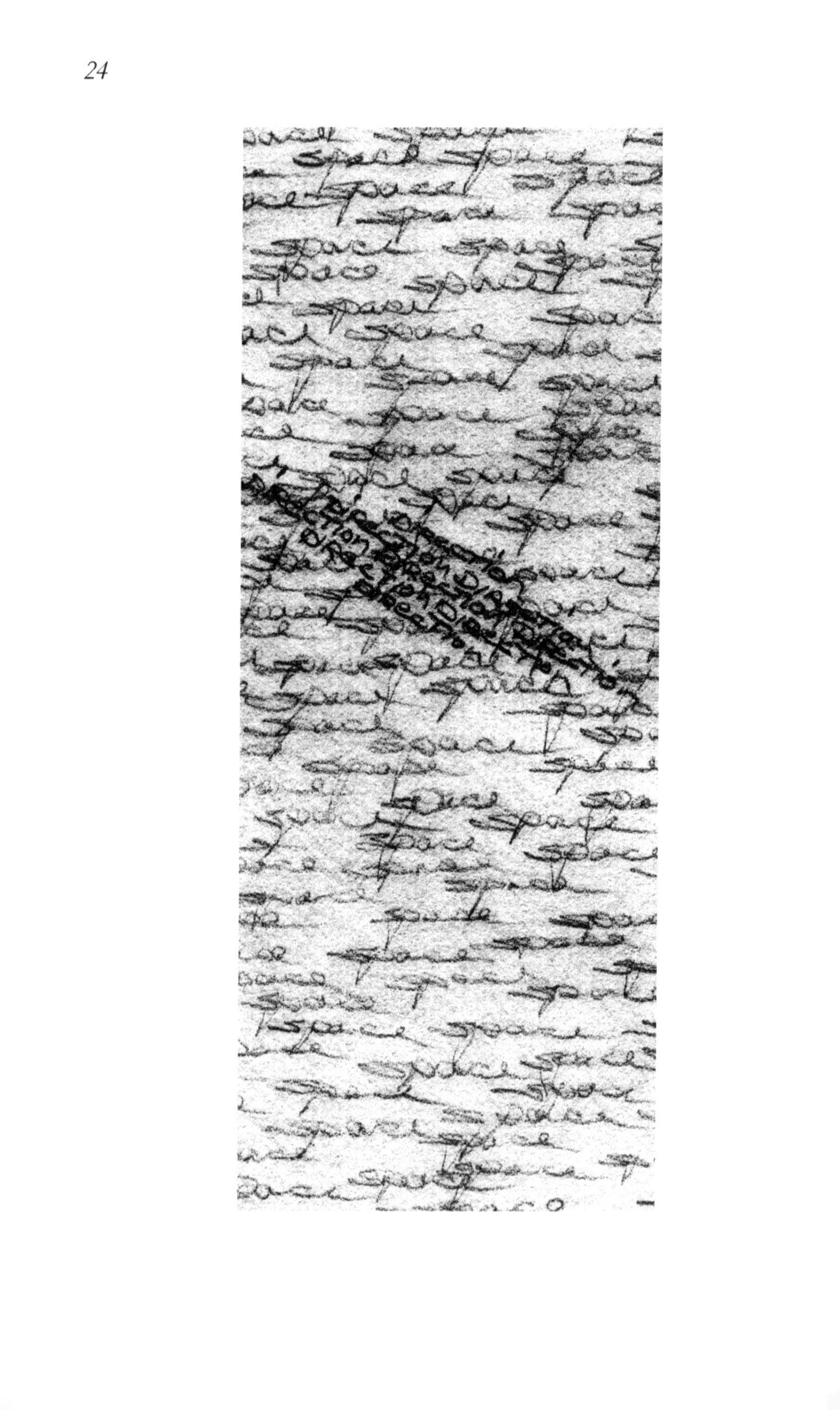

resting
on the way
to purgatory[1]

____

1. "Out beyond ideas of wrongdoing and right-
doing, there is a field. I'll meet you there."
(Rumi)

Easy was a technical assistant that made
clouds disappear with music—pure
platitude. Two literal . . . worlds fare.
Pair of dice found.

Clocks push time . . .
Seconds follow a round position—
We can discuss this tomorrow at the
point of reluctance . . .
What would no words look like? ***then***

Domestication of thought. Don't abuse
an idea. Let it go . . .

You are
judged
by the
language
you keep.

Consumation Soup

dead fur
dead fear
dead cry
dead sound
dead idea
dead form
dead space
dead rat
dead buffalo
dead artist
dead eternity
dead foot
dead hand
dead head
dead hair
dead etc.
dead lust
dead self
dead
pan

the brain is
the organ of retention…
the mind is musical chairs

what would no
words look like?

one might
go so far
as to
say

EXAMPLE

"as is" is only said once upon a time . . .
{lets play chicken with an egg}
language is flesh (the enema within)
    smells evolve . . .

all legs in one basket

a
h
—
y
e
e
!
y
o
u
r
t
o
n
g
u
e
i
s
t
i
e
d
t
o
y
o
u
r
b
o
o
t
s
r
a
p
s

house tears up dog—
going home with a known appendage
held in
proximity—
words change position . . .

(substance abuse)

KISS MY LIPS !
the eternity of
sun
rise—back **rubbbb**
to future plans . . .

HEARTS
BAG
TIME

TIME
is
on my
>**slide**
this is
not a
step

it is queer
tonight!
you can see
to eternity . . .

FORM
is a
reality
NUT

mark my
head
words will
roll . . . mark my head!

—WINDY—
stars all over
the
place

plucking
a raised
eyebrow

dumb
founded—
(position
gathering)

Stars
and
Moons
for-
ever . . .

CARNAL EYES . . .
DALLiANCE
    BLOOMS

LIGHT
GLOWS
IN THE
DARK[1]

---

1. "Zen is the madman yelling: 'If you wanna
tell me that the stars are not words, stop calling
them stars!"

    (Jack Kerouac)

STARS & MOONS
FOREVER—stand and design
youself . . .
six pence & blk. Birds
Do Da—Do Da—[1]

---

1. "If the moon were to say something to the
Earth and the Earth laughed, more people could
be killed than in all the wars put together."

(John Marin by John Marin)

I don't know
if these are
in their

perspective
in a
poin less
universe

lets face it
digestion
takes the
cake . . .

cremation
therapy

YOU!
available
for a
limited time
only . . .

SIDE ?

UFOs may be a figment of
our imagination
GODs may be a fig… of our imagi . . .
even the **UNIVERSE**
may be a fig… of our imagi . . .
WE may be a fig… of our imagi . . .
BUT—
STUPIDITY EXISTS

DISCLAIMER

The words in this volume have been
lifted from previous thoughts—the
words have been re-arranged to protect
the innocent.

[GROOM LAKE RESEARCH FACILITY]

CPSIA information can be obtained
at www.ICGtesting.com
Printed in the USA
LVHW110012221010
634942LV00006B/997/P